American Humane.

Protecting
Children & Animals
Since 1877

American Humane Pet Care Library

Fish

How to

Choose

and

Care

for a

Fish

Laura S. Jeffrey

Enslow Publishers, Inc.

40 Industrial Road	PO Box 38
Box 398	Aldershot
Berkeley Heights, NJ 07922	Hants GU12 6BP
USA	UK

http://www.enslow.com

American Humane.

Protecting
Children & Animals
Since 1877

The American Humane Association is dedicated to preventing the cruelty, abuse, neglect, and exploitation of children and animals. To learn how you can support the vision of a nation where no child or animal will ever be a victim of willful abuse or neglect, visit www.americanhumane.org, phone (303) 792-9900, or write American Humane at 63 Inverness Drive East, Englewood, Colorado, 80112-5117.

Library of Congress Cataloging-in-Publication Data

Jeffrey, Laura S.
    Fish : how to choose and care for a fish / Laura S. Jeffrey.
        p. cm. — (American humane pet care library)
    Summary: Explains how to set up a personalized aquarium, pick the right fish,
        and how to keep them happy and healthy.
    Includes bibliographical references and index.
    ISBN 0-7660-2517-9
    1. Aquarium fishes—Juvenile literature. [1. Aquarium fishes. 2. Fishes. 3. Aquariums. 4. Pets.]
     I. Title.
    SF457.25.J46 2004
    639.34—dc22

                            2003022968

Printed in the United States of America

10 9 8 7 6 5 4 3 2

To Our Readers: We have done our best to make sure all Internet Addresse~ ~~ok were active and appropriate when we went to press. However, the author and the publ~ ~ve no control over and assume no liability for the material available on those Internet sites or ~ other Web sites they may link to. Any comments or suggestions can be sent by e-mail to comments@enslow.com or to the address on the back cover.

Every effort has been made to locate all copyright holders of material used in this book. If any errors or omissions have occurred, corrections will be made in future editions of this book.

Illustration Credits: © 1996–2004 ArtToday, Inc., pp. 3, 5 (right), 8, 9, 11 (right), 12, 15 (left and right), 16, 25, 27, 28, 29, 34, 35, 37 (right), 39; John Bavaro, pp. 42, 43; Corel Corporation, pp. 4, 5 (left), 6, 7 (left), 11 (left), 33 (left), 37 (left); EyeWire, pp. 10, 38, 41 (left); Hemera Technologies, Inc. 1997–2000, pp. 22 (all), 30; Painet, Inc., pp. 13, 14, 19, 23, 26, 33 (right), 40 (top); PhotoDisc, Inc. pp. 1, 7 (right), 18, 41 (right); PhotosForMe.com, pp. 21, 40 (bottom); Courtesy of Cathy Tardosky, pp. 17, 31, 36.

Cover Illustration: Corel Corporation (Horse); PhotoDisc, Inc. (Gerbil, Dog, Fish, Cat, Bird).

Contents

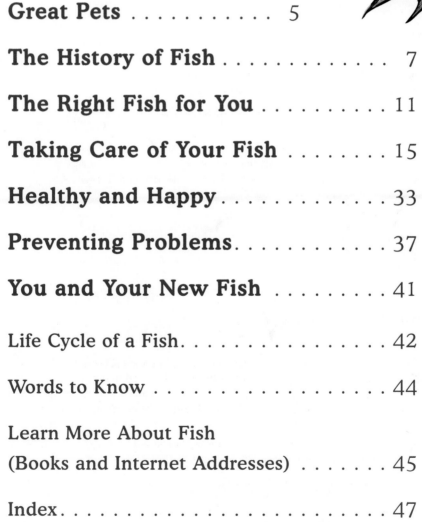

Fish make great pets.

1

Great Pets

 Fish are perhaps the most common of all pets. They are beautiful to look at and fun to watch. A tank full of fish lets people look at nature underwater.

But fish are not easy pets. Because fish live in a different type of environment, you will need to spend a lot of time, energy, and money to take care of your new pet.

This book will help you choose the right fish for you. It will tell you what to feed your new pet and how to keep it healthy and safe. You will learn a lot about what you need to know about caring for your fish.

Fish are fun to watch.

Fish have been pets for many years. Fish farmers in China and Japan began breeding goldfish as pets thousands of years ago.

The History of Fish

 Fish have been pets for many years. In fact, no one knows just when fish became household pets. Goldfish are perhaps the oldest and most common type of pet fish. Fish farmers in China and Japan began breeding goldfish as pets thousands of years ago. Ancient art and books show that goldfish were kept in Asian homes as early as 800 A.D.

Fish swim in a pool in this ancient Chinese artwork.

Goldfish come in many different shapes and sizes.

Goldfish became common household pets in other countries after 1650. This is when European countries began trading goods with Asian countries. At first, goldfish were kept in outside ponds. They became indoor pets sometime during the late 1800s.

Goldfish were first bred in the United States in 1878. Now there are many goldfish farms in the United States. Other types of fish, called tropical fish, are also available as pets.

Today, goldfish come in different sizes and colors. Some goldfish are very small, while others can grow to be more than a foot long.

Fast Fact

Most goldfish live to be about five years old, but some can live as long as fifteen years or more.

Goldfish are a popular first pet. They are easy to take care of.

3

The Right Fish for You

Goldfish are popular "starter pets." They are easy to care for. They do not need as much time and money as other pet fish.

Is a fish the right pet for you?

Once you are a more experienced pet fish owner, you can fill an aquarium with many different kinds of fish. The wide range of colors, sizes, and shapes that fish come in will be fun to watch. A community tank is an aquarium that holds many different kinds of fish. If you decide to have a community tank, you must make sure that all your fish get along well together.

Social, or friendly, types of fish get along well with many different types of fish. Examples of these are danios, tetras, mollies, guppies, and swordtails.

Semisocial types are sometimes friendly. They can be kept with fish of the same size. Examples of semisocial fish are gourami and angelfish.

Fast Fact

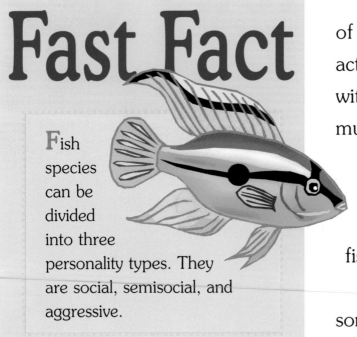

Fish species can be divided into three personality types. They are social, semisocial, and aggressive.

Aggressive types of fish are bold and active. They will fight with other fish. They must be kept by themselves or in pairs. An example of an aggressive fish is a male betta.

Also be aware that some fish lay eggs.

Other fish, such as guppies and mollies, bear live young. If you

Some fish lay eggs. Read about the type of fish you want before deciding which to buy.

get a live-bearing fish, you will need to have hiding places in the tank for the babies, or the larger fish might eat the babies. The babies will need a place to live, too. Be sure your tank is large enough to hold all the fish.

Visit the library to get books on different types of fish. Workers at an aquarium store or a pet store can help you. But just because someone works at a store does not mean he or she is an expert. It is up to you to do some research before you go shopping for your new pet. Ask friends with aquariums about the kinds of fish they have. Once you have fish in your home, it is too late to experiment.

Some fish lay their eggs on the surface of the water. These eggs look like bubbles.

Some fish are hardy and easy to keep. Others are so fragile that they will die if the water temperature in the tank falls a couple of degrees. As a new fish owner, you should choose fish that are easy to care for. That way, your new pet will be able to survive any minor mistakes you may make in the beginning.

4

Taking Care of Your Fish

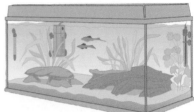

Every year, millions of fish die before their time because they were not cared for properly. When you have the responsibility of caring for any kind of pet, you must give the best possible care.

Before bringing your new fish home, buy all the supplies you need. Unlike some other pets, fish need a lot of supplies. These supplies should be bought and set up before you bring home your new pet.

Before bringing your new fish home, make sure you have everything set up.

Aquariums

An aquarium is a tank with glass or clear plastic walls. Fish are housed in them. A good rule is to buy the largest aquarium that you can afford. Remember you also need room for the aquarium in your home. The more water the aquarium holds, the less it will be affected by outside temperature changes. Avoid using a fishbowl in an unusual shape as an aquarium. It may look nice, but it is not always the best home for your fish.

Avoid fish tanks and fishbowls that are unusual shapes. Horizontal tanks like this one are a good choice.

Fish swim horizontally (across) more often than vertically (up and down). For this reason, do not use a tall, thin aquarium.

Fish have hardly anything to do but swim around. So do not choose fish that are too big for the aquarium you choose. If you do, the fish will feel too crowded. If you get young fish, be sure that once they are grown, they will still fit in with their tank mates and the tank size.

The total inches of fish in your tank should not be more than the number of gallons your tank holds. For example, if you have five tropical fish that are each three inches long,

Fish need room to swim around.

then you have fifteen inches of fish. That means your tank must be able to hold at least fifteen gallons of water. If it does not, you have too many fish for your tank. For goldfish species, it is better to have one gallon of water for every two inches of fish.

Filters

A filter is a tool that takes small debris out of the water. Fish add waste to the water when they eat food. The filter is needed to keep the water clear and safe. An air pump keeps oxygen in the water and helps the filter keep the water clean.

Perhaps the best kind of filter to start with is one that is placed under the gravel. This plastic, slotted

Fast Fact

Did you know that there are over a hundred types of goldfish? Only twenty types are sold today.

tray fits about half an inch from the bottom of the aquarium. An air pump moves the water under the tray and up through the gravel in the tank. Tiny creatures called bacteria live in the gravel. These bacteria eat

If you get a live-bearer fish, you will need room in the tank for the baby fish.

the waste made by the fish. This helps to keep the water clean.

Air Pumps

Air pumps differ in their cost and the amount of air they produce. Some are noisier than others.

Some fish, such as goldfish, like unheated water. But most tropical fish need a water temperature of 70 to 78 degrees Fahrenheit (21 to 25 degrees Celsius). This is hotter than normal room temperature. A heater and thermometer keep the same healthy temperature in the tank. You should buy a heater with about five watts of power rating for each gallon of water. A ten-gallon tank would need a fifty-watt heater.

Lights and Hoods

Your tank should not be kept in direct sunlight. But fish need some light. Buy an artificial light with a cover, or hood, for the top of the tank. The two types of bulbs are fluorescent and incandescent. A fluorescent bulb is better because it is cooler and does not cost

much to run. It also shows off your fish's natural colors better than an incandescent light does.

The hood on the light keeps your fish from jumping out of the tank. It helps keep the water temperature the same. The hood also keeps things from getting into the tank, such as dust, fingers, and cats' paws.

If you do not have room for a big fish tank, think about getting a fishbowl.

If your fishbowl or tank is big enough, you may want to add special decorations. Only add ones that are made just for fishbowls or tanks.

Gravel and Plants

Buy enough gravel to form a one-or two-inch layer over the under-gravel filter. On top of the gravel, you can place plants and other decorations. Make sure whatever you use is safe for your fish. Do not put in any items unless they are made for an aquarium. Even rocks can be harmful to your fish.

Live aquarium plants need strong lighting and good water quality. It is important to start with very healthy plants.

Harmful Chemicals

Most tap water contains chlorine and ammonia. These chemicals can kill your fish. You may need to buy a special chemical to add to the tank water. This chemical will help

Be patient setting up your new tank. Before long, you can watch your new pets swim around.

to keep the water clean by killing the chlorine and ammonia.

Once you have all your supplies, set up your fish's future home. This will allow the water to get to room temperature and get rid of harmful bacteria.

Where Should the Fish Tank Go?

An important decision is where to place the tank in your home. Do not put it in direct sunlight or near a heating or cooling source. That can cause algae to grow and could also change the water temperature. Also, set up the tank near an electrical outlet. Your tank will need at least three electrical sources: one for the light, one for the heater, and one for the pump.

You must be sure about the location of your tank. You also need to be sure that the stand or table the aquarium is on will be strong enough to hold it. Once the tank is put together and filled with water, it will be very heavy and almost impossible to move. Each gallon of water weighs more than eight pounds.

Setting Up the Tank

Rinse the aquarium with tap water and check for leaks. Then rinse everything that is going into the aquarium. Do not use any soaps or cleaning solutions. Even small amounts can be harmful. To protect your fish, have a special bucket and scrubber just for aquarium use.

After rinsing everything off, it is time to set up the aquarium. Put together the under-gravel filter, and place it in the empty tank. Then connect the air tubes to the air pump.

Here are some important parts of your fish tank.

hood

plants

filter

gravel

Add the rinsed gravel to the tank, making slopes and hills to make it look more interesting. Then gently pour tap water onto a saucer placed on the gravel. This keeps the water from disturbing the gravel. You may first need to add a chemical to remove ammonia and chlorine to the tap water.

Fill up the tank three-quarters full. Then put in the decorations. Once you are happy with the decorations, finish filling the tank with water.

Once you get the tank set up, you are ready to buy your fish.

Attach the heater to the middle and back of the tank. In this position, it will not get in the way of the aquarium hood. Wait a few minutes for the thermostat to adjust to the tank temperature. Then plug the heater into the outlet. When the indicator light on the heater turns off, that means the water temperature is ready. By watching the tank thermometer, you can adjust the heater to keep the temperature your fish need.

Take a water sample from your tank to the fish shop. Workers there will check it to be sure the quality is good for the fish you are planning to buy. After the water is checked, it is time to buy your fish and bring them home.

Pet Pointer

Before planting live plants, wait two days. This will allow the temperature and water conditions to be good for the plants.

What to Look for When Buying a Fish

When you go into a shop to buy fish, take a good look around. Are the tanks clean? Do the fish look healthy? Are dead fish floating in the tanks? You also need to ask questions. Does the shop have a replacement policy if a fish dies the first few days after you buy it? If the store does not promise that the fish will stay healthy for at least two weeks after you bring it home, then go to another shop.

Do not buy fish that have been taken from the wild. Coral reefs have been stripped of fish.

Ask where the fish in the store came from. You should buy only fish that have been raised on fish farms. Do not buy fish that have been taken from the wild. Entire coral reefs have been stripped of fish. This destroys nature.

Make sure that any fish you buy look healthy. Healthy fish swim with a purpose. Their fins will be held alert. Healthy fish do not have spots or signs of fungus or bacteria on their bodies. Do not buy a fish if its tail looks like it is in bad shape, or if its body looks like it has a kink in it. Do not buy a fish if it acts differently from other fish in the tank.

Bringing Home Your Fish

The fish you buy will be put into a plastic bag. Take your new fish straight home. Float the bag in the aquarium for five to ten minutes. This lets the water temperatures become the same. Next, open the bag and add tank water until the amount of water in the bag doubles.

Wait another five minutes. Then, gently take the fish out of the bag with a net and

Look for healthy fish by choosing ones that swim with a purpose.

place them in the tank. Do not add water from the bag into the tank. The water in the bag could have harmful germs. Start your tank with a few healthy fish. You can build up the number of fish over the next few weeks.

Feeding Your Fish

All fish do not need the same type of food. Most dry foods come as flakes or pellets. For young or small fish, flakes and pellets can be broken up by rubbing them between your fingers.

Other types of fish food include freeze-dried items.

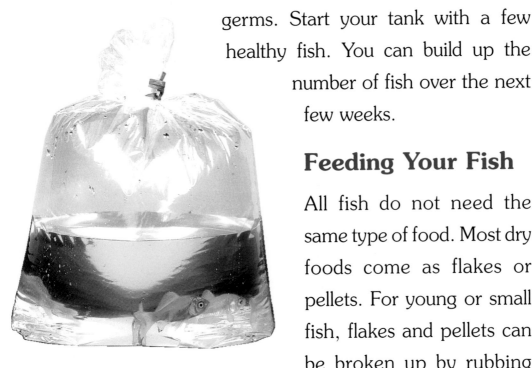

Your new fish will come in a bag. Be sure to get home quickly.

Some larger types of fish may even need to eat live fish. Some fish eat water plants and algae that grow in their surroundings.

Some experts feed their fish twice a day. Others believe that once a day is enough. But everyone agrees that overfeeding a fish is a common but very harmful mistake. Decide on a feeding time for your pets, and try to stick to it.

Fish eat a small amount for their total size. So drop just a pinch or two of food into the

Be sure to feed your fish every day.

tank. If the fish eat all of the food in a few minutes and keep coming to the surface to look for more, add another pinch. Remove any food left over after five minutes. By watching your pets a few times, you will soon learn the correct amount to feed them.

Healthy and Happy

Daily care of your pet fish should include feeding them and watching them to make sure they look healthy. One sick fish can infect all the fish in the aquarium. Make sure that no fish has a sore on its fins or body. Also, make sure there are no fish gasping at the surface of the tank or that a fish has stopped eating. Any of these signs can mean a problem.

Different types of fish need different types of food.

Also, check to see that the filter and air pump are working and that the water temperature in the tank is always the same.

Every week, scrape off the algae on the inside of the aquarium walls, trim dead leaves from the plants, and clean filters, if needed. For goldfish, you should change about a third of the water every week. The water should be at room temperature. You may need to treat the water with special chemicals before placing it in the tank.

If your fish looks sick, check the water quality.

Once a month, gently "vacuum" the gravel in the tank with a special hose that can be bought at a pet supply store. This should remove about a third of the water. Replace this water with treated tap water that is about the same temperature as the water already in the tank.

Fast Fact

Bettas are also called Siamese fightingfish. They are very colorful and will become brighter when excited. Bettas should be kept in separate bowls or tanks.

If you need to remove a sick fish, use a fish net and carefully scoop the fish out.

6

Preventing Problems

 Environmental stress is the leading cause of disease in fish. Environmental stress means that there is a problem in the tank. The problem can be caused by one fish bothering another fish, too many fish in the tank, or leftover food that makes the water dirty. Stress can also be caused by not taking care of the tank, or by smoke or paint fumes getting into the tank.

Too many fish in a tank can hurt the fish.

Stress can cause your fish to eat less or act sick. Be sure to keep pets away from the bowl or tank.

Ich (pronounced *ICK*), or white spot disease, is the most common fish disease. Infected fish have speckles and cysts on their body and fins. Ich can be treated with medicine. But this disease is usually caused by stress, so you should look at the conditions in the tank. One step is to take a small amount of the tank water to the fish shop. Workers there can study the water and tell you if the quality is poor.

Another common fish disease is called velvet. Fish with this disease have a fine, powdery color on them. Velvet affects some types of fish more often than others. It can be hard to treat.

Fish rot is another disease. Fish with this disease look as if their fins are dissolving. Fish rot is usually a sign that the tank water is of very poor quality. The disease can spread quickly, so the problem needs to be taken care of right away.

Remove a fish with fish rot from the tank right away. Move it to a separate container for treatment. Make sure to get the water quality tested so you can learn how to improve it.

Pet Pointer

Ask a veterinarian or fish dealer about other types of illnesses in fish and how to prevent or treat them. By doing this, you will be giving the best possible care for your pet fish.

Watch your fish every day to make sure they remain healthy.

You can have fun watching your new fish.

You and Your New Fish

Whether you have a couple of goldfish or other kinds of fish, a tank is a living environment. Each species of fish has a special place in nature and a way of life that cannot be changed. So think carefully before taking fish as pets. Remember that some fish can live to be fifteen years old. Keep loving and learning more about your pet, and you and your fish will spend many happy years together.

Fish are perhaps the tiniest of pets, but they need a lot of care and attention.

Life Cycle

2.

Only some little fish
become adult fish.

1.

A female fish
lays eggs. Soon
they hatch.

# of a Fish

3.

Some fish can live to be fifteen years old.

Words to Know

aggressive—Ready or willing to start a fight.

aquarium—A tank, usually with glass sides, for housing fish and aquatic plants.

aquatic—Growing or living in or on water.

bacteria—Tiny creatures that cannot be seen with the naked eye. Some bacteria cause disease, while others do good things.

community tank—An aquarium that holds many different kinds of fish.

filter—A device to remove unwanted items from a liquid.

hood—A covering that protects.

semi—Partly. For example, semisocial types of fish are sometimes friendly.

social—Getting along well with others.

Learn More About Fish

Books

Barnes, Julia. *101 Facts About Goldfish.* Milwaukee, Wisc.: Gareth Stevens Pub., 2002.

Coleman, Lori. *My Pet Fish.* Minneapolis, Minn.: Lerner Publications, 1998.

Frost, Helen. *Fish.* Mankato, Minn.: Pebble Books, 2001.

Schwartz, David M. *Fighting Fish.* Milwaukee, Wisc.: Gareth Stevens Pub., 2001.

Internet Addresses

Animaland

<http://www.animaland.org>

Click on Pet Care for more information about the care of different pets.

Just For Kids

<http://www.americanhumane.org/kids/fish.htm>

Find out more about fish on this site from the American Humane Association.

Index